Scary States (of Mind)

Horror in New Jersey

by Alex Giannini

Consultant: Debbie Felton
Professor of Classics
University of Massachusetts
Amherst, Massachusetts

I0808303

Bearport Publishing
Minneapolis, Minnesota

Credits

Cover, © Kim Jones, © Andrew F. Kazmierski/Shutterstock, © LMcCabe/Shutterstock, and © Karl Weller/Shutterstock; 3, Andrew F. Kazmierski; 4-5, © Kim Jones, © Mike Ver Sprill/Shutterstock, and © Malivan_Iuliia/Shutterstock; 6, © Oakland Tribune/Associated Press/Public Domain; 7, © Everett Historical/Shutterstock; 8, © Everett Historical/Shutterstock; 8-9, © Anna Vaczi/Shutterstock; 10-11, © Dawn J Benko/Shutterstock; 11 (inset), © Rtsanderson/Wikimedia Commons/Creative Commons; 12, Philadelphia Newspaper/Wikimedia Commons/Public Domain; 13, © Sky Cinema/Shutterstock; 14, © Everett Historical/Shutterstock; 15, © Andrew F. Kazmierski/Shutterstock; 16, © Tapui/Shutterstock; 17, © Erin Cadigan/Shutterstock and © Pikul Noorod/Shutterstock; 18T, © Intarapong/Shutterstock; 18B, © Mike Flippo/Shutterstock; 19, © Daniel Case/Wikimedia Commons/Creative Commons; 20, © Phant/Shutterstock; 21, © Daniel Case/Wikimedia Commons/Creative Commons; 22, © zef art/Shutterstock; 23, © Jorge Moro/Shutterstock; and 24, © SS1001/Shutterstock.

President: Jen Jenson
Director of Product Development: Spencer Brinker
Editor: Allison Juda
Designer: Micah Edel
Cover: Kim Jones

Library of Congress Cataloging-in-Publication Data

Names: Giannini, Alex, author.
Title: Horror in New Jersey / by Alex Giannini.
Description: Minneapolis Minnesota : Bearport Publishing Company, 2021. | Series: Scary states (of mind) | Includes bibliographical references and index.
Identifiers: LCCN 2020000523 (print) | LCCN 2020000524 (ebook) | ISBN 9781647470777 (library binding) | ISBN 9781647470876 (ebook)
Subjects: LCSH: Haunted places—New Jersey—Juvenile literature. | Ghosts—New Jersey—Juvenile literature. | New Jersey—Miscellanea—Juvenile literature.
Classification: LCC BF1472.U6 G52533 2021 (print) | LCC BF1472.U6 (ebook) | DDC 133.109749—dc23
LC record available at https://lccn.loc.gov/2020000523
LC ebook record available at https://lccn.loc.gov/2020000524

Copyright © 2021 Bearport Publishing Company. All rights reserved. No part of this publication may be reproduced in whole or in part, stored in any retrieval system, or transmitted in any form or by any means, electronic, mechanical, photocopying, recording, or otherwise, without written permission from the publisher.

For more information, write to Bearport Publishing, 5357 Penn Avenue South, Minneapolis, MN 55419. Printed in the United States of America.

CONTENTS

Horror in New Jersey

The Jersey Shore draws millions of visitors every year for summertime fun and sun. But there are horrors hidden across the Garden State, too. Beware of spooky spots like a haunted naval base and a **cursed** tree. Be sure to watch out for a devil hiding in the woods!

Get ready to read four terrifying tales about New Jersey. Turn the page . . . if you dare.

A HAUNTED HISTORY

Lakehurst Naval Air Station, Lakehurst

On May 6, 1937, the *Hindenburg* **airship** was set to arrive at Lakehurst Naval Air Station. It was said to be the largest and safest airship ever built. But the *Hindenburg* never touched down on the runway.

Just before landing, the giant aircraft burst into flames and crashed to the ground! The disaster killed 36 people.

The *Hindenburg* was a dirigible. Unlike a hot-air balloon, a dirigible is powered and can be steered.

The *Hindenburg* airship in flames

Survivors were rushed to the hospital on the base. The burned bodies of the dead were kept in **hangar** number one.

Hindenburg crash survivors

Today, **paranormal** activity is said to take place both in the hospital and in hangar one. Mysterious footsteps echo through the corridors. Voices can be heard at all hours. One worker even felt an invisible hand on his shoulder. Are these the restless spirits of those who lost their lives that day?

The Devil in the Woods

The Pine Barrens, southeastern New Jersey

The Pine Barrens is a large forest that stretches across southeastern New Jersey. These dark woods might be home to a frightening devil.

In 1735, Deborah Leeds was pregnant with her 13th child. Angry that her husband did little to help the family, Deborah yelled out, "Let this one be a devil!" She may have gotten her wish.

The Pine Barrens is filled with ruins, ghost towns, and other creepy spots.

As the legend goes, the child grew horns, hooves, and claws. Black wings **sprouted** from his back. Then, he flew up the chimney and **vanished** into the woods.

After hundreds of sightings in 1909, schools closed to keep students safe and a $10,000 reward was offered to capture the Jersey Devil. To this day, the monster remains on the loose.

A drawing of the Jersey Devil

The Pine Barrens from above

The Pine Barrens is called the most haunted forest in America. It has an area of over 1 million acres (400,000 ha). That's a lot of land where a devil might hide!

Haunted Spy House

Seabrook-Wilson Homestead, Port Monmouth

The Seabrook-Wilson Homestead was a tavern during the Revolutionary War (1775–1783). But it was more than it seemed. The tavern owner listened to British soldiers' conversations. Then, he told the Colonial army the British secrets. That's how the homestead earned its first nickname: The Spy House.

The Seabrook-Wilson Homestead

In the 1970s, the house was turned into a museum. That's when strange activities began. Some visitors saw the spirits of children playing outside. Upstairs, a rocking chair creaked back and forth as the ghostly figure of an old man appeared. Ghost hunters collected enough evidence to give the homestead another nickname: America's Most Haunted House.

One visitor to the museum saw a young boy looking out from an upstairs window. But according to a museum **curator**, the building was empty.

A Picnic Under a Cursed Tree

The Devil's Tree, Bernards Township

A giant oak tree rises up in the middle of an empty field in Bernards Township. Stories about the Devil's Tree are eerie.

In 1900, a local farmer and his family picnicked underneath the oak. But this happy outing had a tragic end. As the story goes, the farmer went mad and killed his entire family.

The Devil's Tree

Overcome by **regret**, the farmer hanged himself from a branch of the giant oak. Since that time, people say the tree is cursed.

Over the years, some people have tried to cut down the tree. But the oak has survived every attempt. However, those who tried to cut it down are said to be cursed.

Visitors say the tree feels warm to the touch all year. In winter, snow melts when it falls on the branches.

Officials put a chain-link fence around the tree to protect it—and those who might come near.

Spooky Spots in New Jersey

GLOSSARY

airship (AIR-ship) a large balloon with engines and a passenger compartment attached; the balloon is filled with a gas that is lighter than air to lift the airship off the ground

curator (KYOO-ray-tur) a person in charge of all or part of a museum

cursed (KURST) under an evil spell and therefore likely to cause evil or injury

hangar (HANG-ur) a shelter for housing and repairing aircrafts

paranormal (pa-ruh-NOR-muhl) events that are not able to be scientifically explained

regret (ri-GRET) to be sorry or sad about something

sprouted (SPROUT-id) grew

vanished (VAN-ishd) disappeared

INDEX

READ MORE

Markovics, Joyce. *Chilling Cemeteries (Tiptoe Into Scary Places).* New York: Bearport (2017).

Phillips, Dee. *Nightmare in the Hidden Morgue (Cold Whispers II).* New York: Bearport (2017).

LEARN MORE ONLINE

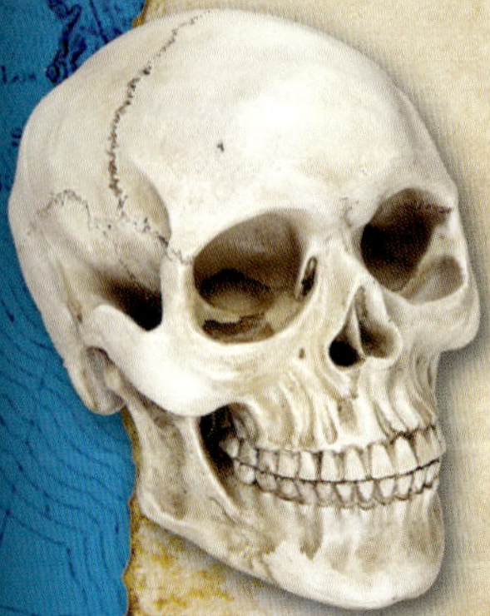

1. Go to **www.factsurfer.com**
2. Enter "**Horror in New Jersey**" into the search box.
3. Click on the cover of this book to see a list of websites.

ABOUT THE AUTHOR

Alex Giannini is a writer who also works in a public library. In his free time, he likes to hunt for thrilling ghost stories.